9 top The Bay Bridge links San Francisco with Oakland. Although four times as long as the Golden Gate, it has never achieved the same legendary status. Even would-be suicides give it a wide berth: only a hundred fatal leaps have occurred here, compared with the thousand from the Golden Gate Bridge.

I f you had to pick one word to describe California, just one that would sum up its very essence, that word would have to be "pioneering." Once upon a time, of course, California was literally full of pioneers—hardy Spanish, English, and Russian settlers trying to stake their claim upon a land already populated by American Indians. Until the railroads and other modes of transportation made the travel to California easier, the rigors of the journey kept away all but the strongest, bravest and most determined. Today, in many ways, California is still the frontier—but the new ground that is being broken is conceptual, not literal. This is true in medicine, theology, physics, psychology, business, technology— even sports. For instance, the inclusion of mountain bicycling in the 1996 Olympics owes largely to the enthusiasm of the Californians who defined, refined and championed the sport.

New trends are always coming from California and sweeping their way East. Think of health food, yoga, mind-body medicine, the men's movement, Apple computers and yes, even computer hacking. It's no coincidence that much of the flower-child, "Make love, not war" ambiance that defined the 1960s came out of Haight-Ashbury and Berkeley in the San Francisco Bay area, and that much of the New Age sensibility that is beginning to percolate through mainstream culture first took hold in trendy Los Angeles. The multimillion-dollar human potential movement also owes much to California, particularly to Esalen, that fabled oceanside retreat center in Big Sur, which has served as a mecca for the personal-growth set.

Where else but in Esalen could you expect to soak in a sulfurous communal hot tub overlooking the Pacific Ocean and watch several nude masseuses on an adjoining deck kneading the flesh of their equally nude clients? And where else but in California (at the UC Berkeley School of Medicine, to be precise), could you find yourself at a party organized by graduating medical students to commemorate the spirits of the dead cadavers they had come to know so well? Columbus, Ohio? Not likely. A theme party like this may not catch on back East, but it does speak to a decidedly fresh and slightly quirky approach to life that defines the California spirit.

When most out-of-staters think of California, they invariably tend to think of Hollywood, or the beaches, and the wild life at play there: the

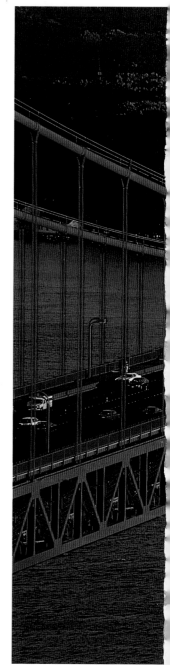

CONTENTS

winsome young things in leopard-skin thongs, the tan young Hercules in brightly-colored jams. But while the cult of the body is very strong in California (rumors have it there are more massage therapists per square mile than appliance repairmen), the state can lay claim to a strong intellectual life, too. Some of the brightest film visionaries, such as George Lucas, are experimenting with multimedia and devising new ways to marry high technology and entertainment. One day soon, the multimedia revolution might take over the classroom, if its current crop of inventors can just figure out how

11 top Considered by many to be California's most "laid-back" city, San Diego is a stone's throw from the desert, yet cooled by ocean breezes that yield balmy days and comfortable evenings. The city is embellished by restored Spanish-style homes and buildings that stand in stark contrast to its modern-day skyscrapers.

11 bottom The towering giants forged from concrete, glass, and steel in San Francisco's Financial District show one aspect of the city. Views of the bay and ocean, homes clinging to hillsides, spacious parks and museums are among its more appealing features.

to turn a buck with it. Other great minds, such as Harvard-trained scientist Gary Zukav, author of the award-winning The *Dancing Wu Lei Masters* (which covered the new physics) and his more recent book, *Seat of The Soul*, are tracing the connection between physics and mysticism. And a growing number of health professionals, including miracle-worker/cardiologist Dean Ornish, M.D., are changing the way Americans think about the mind as an agent of health or disease.

As these few examples illustrate, Californians are still very much on the frontier, and will continue to be so, in ways that are certain to influence the rest of the nation for some time to come. Why California is such fertile territory for new thought and new technologies is anyone's guess, but maybe such inventiveness is solar-powered, or inspired by majestic landscapes, vast open spaces, primeval forests, or pounding surf, all of which you'll find in abundance in the Golden State.

12-13 South of Carmel lies scenic Point Lobos State Reserve (pictured here is a stretch of the shore close to Cannery Point). The reserve is popular with nature lovers who, from December to March, use its dramatic vantage points to watch for migrating whales.

13 top and bottom The coastline between Point Lobos Reserve and Point Sur is characterized by rocks emerging from frothing surf and almost vertical cliffs, formed by mountains of the Santa Lucia range as they plunge down to meet the sea. The unspoiled scenery draws visitors from all over who are impressed with its inspiring beauty.

14 and 15 Cradled
between the Sierra
Nevada and the
Inyo Mountains,
Owens Valley owes
its wilderness
landscape to the
absence of rainfall.

When a diversion of
water to Los Angeles
caused Owens Lake
to dry up, an arid
and desolate valley
with little or no
vegetation was left
in its place.

The Merced River running through
Yosemite Valley

An aerial view of San Francisco

The Pacific coast of Southern
California

Redwood National Park

18-19 In recent years, downtown Los Angeles has undergone a rapid process of urban renewal: the construction of shopping malls, an elaborate Music Center complex and many high-end hotels has revitalized the area and given a new look to this part of the city.

20-21 Yosemite National Park is a spectacular sight in any season but especially when it lies under a blanket of snow. At this time of year skiing and hiking with snowshoes become immensely popular.

Zabriskie Point in Death Valley

Los Angeles at dusk

Oregon

Lake Goose

Lake Eagle

Lake Honey

Mount Klamath

Lassen Volcanic National Park

Sacramento

Lake Tahoe

Lake Clear

Santa Rosa

Napa Valley

Richmond

Sacramento

Sierra

Berkeley

San Francisco

Oakland

Silicon Valley

San Joaquin

Santa Cruz

Mono Lake

Kings Canyon National Park

Sequoia National Park

Nevada

Nevada

Mount Whitney

Death Valley

Monterey

Big Sur

Pacific Ocean

Morro Bay

San Luis Obispo

Mojave Desert

Santa Barbara

San Miguel

Santa Cruz

Ventura

Los Angeles

Joshua Tree National Monument

Santa Rosa

Santa Monica

San Bernardino

Colorado

Long Beach

Pasadena

San Nicholas

Palm Springs

Salton Sea

Channel Islands

Santa Catalina

San Diego

San Clemente

Mexico

*T*here are many stories about how California came to receive such a musical name, but here is just one. Andrew F. Rolle, author of *California, A History*, claims that California was named for an imaginary island of the same name which 16th-century Spanish writer Garci Ordonez de Montalvo wrote about in *Las Sergas de Esplandian* (The Exploits of Esplandian). In de Montvalo's imagination, California was a wild and craggy "island full of gold, inhabited by ebony-skinned Amazons," ruled by a pagan queen named Calafia. This mythic island existed somewhere

22 top The Native Americans who came into contact with the first Europeans were essentially peace-loving people: tribal dances had a social role but also marked sacred and seasonal passages in the community's life.

between the Indies and a "Terrestrial Paradise." The Spanish writer's account was so believable (or at least, compelling) that he had others convinced that it really did exist.

The book was at the height of its popularity when Hernando-Cortes and his men were seeking the legendary northwestern sea passage to the Indies and its riches. They had hopes of finding the legendary California as well. Navigator Juan Rodriguez Cabrillo was the first to arrive here, from New Spain, as Mexico was then known. He came ashore in 1542 and found peaceful Native American people instead of fierce Amazons, but not the hoped-for gold. Cabrillo landed in San Diego Bay in September 1542 and a month later reached the site of the present-day Ventura to the north. Initially seeking a route to the East by sailing northward, Cabrillo's expedition along the coast was also intended to explore and conquer. The navigator and his crew sailed as far as the present-day Monterey and Fort Ross, before furious winter winds forced them to turn back.

The Spanish did not vigorously colonize California in those years, but merely used a handful of sites on the seaboard as supply and support bases for ships sailing to the Philippines, then under Spanish rule. No settlers arrived here in 1579 either, when the British explorer and "privateer," Sir Francis Drake, anchored in a bay just north of modern San Francisco to claim the land for England. Drake

22 bottom Dressed in furs and wearing snow shoes so they could move quickly and stealthily even in fresh snow, many Native Americans made their livelihood from hunting. As can be seen from this woodcut— done by Eduard Vermorcken from a drawing by George Catlin (1796-1872)— a prime quarry was the buffalo. Millions of bison once roamed the wilds of North America.

22-23 This French print shows California natives armed with bows and arrows, which they carry wrapped in animal skins. In the traditional state of "undress" and hair pulled up in a top knot, a native poses with bow and arrow while his tribesman looks on.

23 top These young Native American hunters made a notable impression on the first Europeans to settle in the San Francisco Bay area. The natives' rituals were elaborate, yet their lifestyle was simple and respectful of the earth.

25 This map,
printed in France in
1634, shows that
California was little
known at the time
and was mistakenly
thought to be an
island.

24 top The ships of Sir
Francis Drake,
"privateer"
commissioned by Queen
Elizabeth I. In 1579 he
sailed the length of the
California Coast,
weighing anchor off
Marin County to
shelter from stormy seas.

24 bottom left A map
of America dating
from 1686 is exhibited
in Rotterdam's
Maritime Museum.
By that date
California had
already been
"discovered" by
Europeans, but it
would be almost a
hundred years more
before the missions of
the Camino Real
would be founded.

24 bottom right A
portrait of Sir Francis
Drake, whose
expeditions were
aimed at challenging
Spain's supremacy as
a sea power. In 1579
he was the first
Englishman to sight
the coast of
California.

named the surrounding lands New
Albion and his contact with Native
Americans convinced him that—
despite their painted faces and tribal
dances—their intentions were friendly.

Partly because of California's
inaccessibility, the Spanish did not
start to settle the territory until nearly
200 years later. In 1769 Father
Junipero Serra arrived here from
Mexico with a military expedition led
by Don Gaspar de Portola. In the
space of 50 years, this Franciscan friar
established 21 missions along the
coast of what was known as Upper
(or Alta) California—as distinguished
from Lower or Baja California. His
vigor was matched, in the political
field, by that of Portola, who was
appointed the region's governor. The
route Serra followed northward in
founding missions was called El
Camino Real (The Royal Road) and,
later, the Old Spanish Trail. The same
route is now traveled by the almost
equally legendary Highway 101,
which winds the entire length of
California, from the Mexican border
to the far north.

26 top left An old print illustrating the first national exhibition held at Mission Dolores in San Francisco. Even today the mission remains the heart of the city.

26-27 *The Presidio in San Francisco, shown in a print by Ludovic Khoris, was established by the Spanish conquistadors in 1776 as a military garrison. The building and surrounding area have now been designated a national park.*

27 top *Native Americans with ornately painted bodies perform a traditional Indian dance in front of Mission Dolores in San Francisco. This illustration, also by Ludovic Khoris (1822), is from Otto von Kotzebue's book* A New Voyage Round the World.

The first mission was built at San Diego. Native Americans were "converted" to Christianity and were set to work on irrigation and building projects under working conditions that approached slavery. In contrast to the actions of the conquistadors in Mexico, however, little Native American blood was shed. For military defense, the Spanish built garrisoned forts called "presidios" at strategic locations in San Diego, Santa Barbara, Monterey and San Francisco. Another element of Spanish colonization strategy was the establishment of "pueblos," planned settler communities that laid claim to territories and were the base for the acquisition of more land. Pueblos were founded in San Jose, Santa Cruz, and, in 1781, Los Angeles. In all, the 21 missions stretching from San Diego to Sonoma enabled travelers to safely cover a distance of 500 miles without carrying provisions.

When Mexico became independent of Spain in 1821, the Californios, as the Mexican-Spanish settlers were called, declared their loyalty to Mexico. As a consequence, the Mexican governors secularized the missions and parceled out the mission ranches to former military officials and other favored individuals. The Native Americans were "liberated" and driven off the mission settlements. The ensuing land grants created huge ranches (up to 50,000 acres), mainly for cattle raising, whose owners became the "aristocratic" class of this territory. During the period of Spanish and Mexican colonization, contacts with the Yankee inhabitants of American soil were sporadic, dependent on occasional trading ships that arrived from New England. Later trappers came overland across the Sierra Nevada, journeying across the Great Valley following the two rivers that flowed into San Francisco Bay. American Jedediah Smith led an expedition to this region in 1826 and described a land prolific with animals. Earlier, in 1812, Russians, too, had descended from Alaska to hunt otters and had built Fort Ross along the northern coast as a trading and fur-trapping center.

But wildlife was not all the territory had to offer. When Smith set up a fortified base camp of his Rocky Mountain Fur Company—on the shores of the American River, close to Mono Lake—it is said that someone noticed a dazzling gleam from pebbles in the water. It was gold . . . but no one yet realized its significance. The trappers preferred to continue their journey south and

27 bottom right *Junipero Serra, Franciscan friar, is regarded as the founding father of California. The Spanish believed that once they had converted the Native Americans to Christianity, the natives would no longer resist the occupation of their land.*

27 center right *In 1678 the Jesuits arrived in California, accompanying an expedition led by Francisco de Lucenilla. The conflicting goals of the participants soon became all too clear: for some it was conversion of the natives, for others acquisition of land and riches for the Spanish crown.*

eventually reached San Diego. Here the Mexican government politely requested that they return, in no uncertain terms.

The name that would eventually be linked with the gold rush was not Smith but Sutter. Hoping to build a self-sustaining colony in the Sacramento Valley, the Swiss-born John (Johann) Sutter—a businessman who has been called a "dreamer with a gifted tongue"—managed to acquire a 44,000-acre tract of land near the junction of the American and the Sacramento rivers, close to the overland routes. At the site of California's future capital, he built a fort—soon a well-known trading post for furs and provisions—set up a sawmill and called the place New Helvetia. For $30,000 the enterprising Sutter also bought the contents of Fort Ross from the Russians, who departed California in 1841. Much to the irritation of the Mexican authorities, who adamantly wished to discourage immigration, Sutter welcomed American newcomers entering the region from the Sierra Nevada.

As the Mexicans feared, the California territories held an irresistible appeal for the U.S. government, which had been expanding its own borders since winning independence from Britain. Reaching the Pacific Ocean looked to then-president Polk like a natural sequence of events, part of the young country's "manifest destiny." The English, too, did not hide their

28 left and bottom right California was not only the promised land for gold-seekers but for trappers as well. According to Jedediah Smith, who led an expedition to the region in 1826, these territories teemed with animal life, seemingly there for the killing.

28 top right Johann August Sutter, a California pioneer on whose land gold was first discovered in 1848, did not profit from the discovery. Dazzled by the hope of becoming rich, thousands of prospectors soon overran the fertile land that he intended to be occupied by hard-working farmers

29 top This photograph, taken in 1893, shows the capture of a grizzly bear. The bear was the motif on the flag of the Republic of California, hoisted by the state's settlers in 1846.

29 bottom Before gold fever took hold, New Helvetia, founded by Sutter, was a peaceful paradise for would-be settlers in California. The discovery of a nugget of gold in the American River radically changed the course of events.

30 top A cowhand drives a herd of cattle, a major source of income once the gold boom ended and left thousands of fortune-hunters penniless.

interest in a possible annexation.
From 1843-46 Captain John C.
Fremont led two U.S. government
surveying expeditions into California.
As part of the "scientific" purpose of
the expedition, Fremont's project
succeeded in carefully mapping the
overland routes—a great boon to
future settlers.

In May of 1846, the United
States went to war with Mexico over
Texas. A month later, a group of U.S.
citizens hoisted the new Bear Flag (a
grizzly bear facing a red star on a
white background) at Sonoma, north
of San Francisco, declaring the
existence of the independent
Republic of California. The revolution
was short lived. Soon afterward U.S.
forces under Commodore Robert F.
Stockton and General Stephen Watts
Kearny easily conquered California.
Ill-defended Monterey was taken

31 bottom A San
Francisco saloon,
packed with gold
hunters in search of
entertainment.
Today the heady
atmosphere of the
Gold Rush days is re-
created in several
bars in the city,
mainly in the North
Beach neighborhood.

32 top On September 9, 1850, California joined the Union, an event celebrated in San Francisco in grand style on October 29 of that same year. Although the city never earned the distinction of becoming the state capital, it gained in immortality thanks to the gold boom.

32 left On July 16, 1846, John Charles Fremont occupied Monterey as a representative of the U.S. government in California. Soon afterward he raised the Union flag in San Diego and Los Angeles, which was then a small village.

without firing a shot, and San Francisco fell just as readily. In 1848, Mexico officially transferred California to the United States. The northern boundary of California, along the 42nd parallel, as well as the boundary shared with Nevada, were set that same year.

The Mexicans soon had time to rue their loss. In January 1848, just days before the treaty was signed, the California Gold Rush began when James Marshall, an employee at Sutter's sawmill, spied gold in the waters of the American River. Sutter did his best to keep the discovery quiet, but the news leaked out. San Francisco papers published the word and soon people were reading about it from as far away as Hawaii and Australia. In May 1848 the San Francisco newspaper, *The Californian*, suspended publication since "the majority of our subscribers and many of our advertisers have closed their doors and places of business and left town" for the Sierra in the frenzied quest for gold.

32-33 The heroic days of the early West were celebrated in numerous prints. This one, inspired by a poster dated 1875, illustrates a wagon train on a rigorous journey across the mountains of North America.

33 top left A ubiquitous presence in stories of the American West, including California, the legendary cowboy was said to be quick on the draw in the lawless frontier towns.

33 top right At this bar in Sacramento, "capital" of the Gold Rush, prospectors, laborers, and others flocked to a saloon to spend their earnings.

In no time at all, the Gold Rush of 1849 was under way. A mile-wide vein of quartz-bearing gold started from Sutter's land and stretched for 160 miles, as far as Mariposa. Paradoxically, the discovery that brought riches to others meant ruin for Sutter. In the wake of the ensuing chaos, his workers quit their jobs, horses were stolen, and fields and livestock were abandoned by farmers turned gold-seekers. A migration of biblical proportions brought an influx of some 100,000 or more fortune seekers to California. Aspiring millionaires set forth on long and strenuous journeys over land and sea. Some circumnavigated South America; others disembarked in Panama to make their way through the jungle of the isthmus by canoe or on foot. Tens of thousands came overland by wagon, horse, mule, or by foot, in the infernal heat of desert regions and icy cold of the mountains. The region quickly became populated by prospectors who wandered from place to place with little to their names but tools with which to dig and pan for gold. Even the landscape was changed, as miners diverted streams, and later, when more efficient hydraulic methods washed whole hillsides away.

Within the space of two years, from 1848 to 1850, California's population had swelled nearly 500% (or as much as 2000%, according to some estimates). At the same time the territory rapidly achieved statehood. When California joined the Union in 1850 as the 31st state, it did so as a nonslavery or "free" state, having had its own constitution and governor since October 10, 1849.

Just as California's rapid rise to statehood owed much to the gold boom, so did the origin of San Francisco as a major city. Those who permanently settled there were not only gold-diggers who struck it rich and stayed, but also individuals who opted to try other lines of business. In the early days of the gold rush, San Francisco grew from a small village to a "city" almost overnight. An immense encampment of tents and wooden shacks sprouted up— inhabited mainly by males aged 20 to 30, who came to town to spend their nuggets on food, drink, and women. As in many Gold Rush boom towns, law and order (or lack thereof) was an enormous problem.

35 top left A stream is diverted in the hopes of revealing gold.

35 top right Nearly 100,000 "Forty-Niners" arrived in California in 1849 to sieve the sand of Sacramento and the rivers and streams of the Sierra Nevada.

36-37, 36 top and 37 center right San Francisco's charm is derived in large part from the steeply pitched streets and the Victorian homes built by the city's wealthy citizens.

By 1865 California's "mother lode" in the Sierra Nevada foothills had yielded more than 750 million dollars in gold. When the supply of gold declined, the discovery of silver provided new support for the city's growth. Mining silver, however, was a different matter: it called for investment of capital, not improvised, go-it-alone adventurism. It meant industry and organization. An orderly plan for the layout of the city was drawn up, inspired by the grid pattern that characterizes the streets of New York. Fortunately it did not include the hills, since the less direct routes subsequently taken to their peaks are still one of the city's most attractive features.

Californians had taken a stand against slavery in their constitution. Unaffected by the Civil War, California's problem was not

abolition of slavery but regulation of immigration. For example, a law of 1850, later repealed, imposed a $20 tax for every foreign worker. Tens of thousands of Chinese immigrants played a major role in the construction of the railroads, including the Central Pacific that connected Chicago with California. Work began in 1863, five years after the Union Pacific Railroad had crossed the Sierra Nevada at Donner Pass (named after the ill-fated pioneers of the same name). In 1869 the Central Pacific joined the Union Pacific coming from Nebraska. With

38 center Men
employed by the
Northern Pacific
railroad pose in front
of the locomotive on
which they traveled to
their work site. They
were building part of
the northern
railroad line that
connected the state of
Washington with
Minnesota.

38-39 Chinese
workers helped turn
California into a
modern state. Here a
group of Chinese
laborers (shown
wearing the
traditional wide-
brimmed hats)

prepare the terrain
for the tracks that
took the railroad
through the granite
mountains of the
Sierra Nevada, from
Sacramento to
Promontory Point,
Utah.

39 top May 10,
1869, marked the
completion of the
transcontinental
railroad linking the
Mississipi Valley and
the Pacific Coast.
This picture shows the
meeting of the Union
Pacific and Central
Pacific lines at
Promontory Point,
Utah. The occasion

was celebrated with a
ceremony during
which the last spike,
made out of gold, was
fixed in place. The
colossal construction
venture had far-
reaching effects on
the local economies of
the areas it passed
through.

38 bottom Chinese
immigrants worked hard
to build the railways
through wilderness areas.
Their arrival in large
numbers compensated for
the shortage of local
manpower but eventually
led to a backlash. At the
end of the 19th century,
Congress passed
legislation to stop the flow
of immigrants from Asia.

the last ceremonial golden spike was
driven, Atlantic and Pacific met,
making California vastly more
accessible. Now travelers could make
the journey of more than 3,000 miles
from coast to coast in less than seven
days.

The state's population had
grown by a further half million by
1875, the year that marked the start
of a recession. One of the results was
the closure of the Bank of California
for lack of liquid funds. When
recovery eventually came, it was
thanks to agriculture. An ideal
climate and fertile land proved great
allies. Italian immigrants also did
their part: the vineyards they planted
were the first chapter in the Napa
Valley success story. California had by
then moved into the 20th century,
but an unseen and fearsome force lay
in wait beneath the ground.

On April 17, 1906, an
earthquake rocked San Francisco for
48 long seconds. The huge fires that

39 right An 1870 poster, boasting "San Francisco to New York in 6 days and 20 hours," advertised the new railroad links between the Pacific and Atlantic Coasts, which made the Wild West vastly more accessible.

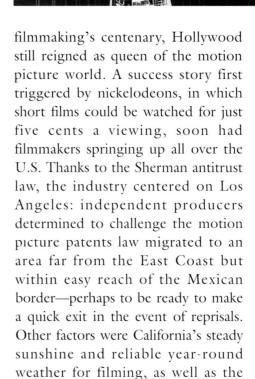

followed left 28,000 buildings in ashes. The whole U.S. rallied behind the city, with money poured into the reconstruction effort by the state and by magnates like Rockefeller. There have been other quakes since then, but relatively few victims.

Before nature does her worst, one of California's most noted protagonists of the 20th century—the film industry—doubtless has many thrills and pleasures in store for us. In 1995 as the world celebrated

filmmaking's centenary, Hollywood still reigned as queen of the motion picture world. A success story first triggered by nickelodeons, in which short films could be watched for just five cents a viewing, soon had filmmakers springing up all over the U.S. Thanks to the Sherman antitrust law, the industry centered on Los Angeles: independent producers determined to challenge the motion picture patents law migrated to an area far from the East Coast but within easy reach of the Mexican border—perhaps to be ready to make a quick exit in the event of reprisals. Other factors were California's steady sunshine and reliable year-round weather for filming, as well as the availability of cheap labor.

In the 1920s filmmaking was in its first heyday, with names like D.W. Griffith, Charlie Chaplin, and Cecil B. De Mille coming to the fore. Griffith "invented" such techniques as the camera close-up, scenic long

42 top left
Originally erected in
San Francisco's
Lincoln Park in
1908, the imposing
Cliff House offers
fine views of the

coast: on a clear day
you can see the
Farallon Islands,
more than 30 miles.
away. The rocks in
the background are
home to sea lions.

42 top right Market
Street, in San
Francisco's Financial
District, in an old
photo. At the time,
horses and buggies
and cable cars

carried residents
around the city.
Market Street runs
on the diagonal
across the orderly
grid layout of San
Francisco streets.

42 center The Palace
of Fine Arts, built for
the Panama-Pacific
Exposition of 1915,
has long dominated
the cityscape of San
Francisco: its
unmistakable
structure, with domes
and neoclassical
colonnades, extends
over a wide area.

42 bottom An ocean
liner berths in San
Diego harbor after
sailing from New
York via the Panama
Canal. The city is a
popular tourist
destination, but
maritime trade and
shipping form a
major element of the
city's economy, along
with the presence of
the largest U.S.
naval base in the
Pacific.

43 top An old picture of Mann's Chinese Theatre (then Grauman's Chinese), a Los Angeles landmark on Hollywood Boulevard. Known for its film-star "Walk of Fame," the unusual edifice opened in 1927 with the screening of a film produced by Cecil B. De Mille.

43 botton Spring Street , Los Angeles, from a photograph taken in 1910. The village had by now become a city and Spring Street was the site of Los Angeles's first building to exceed three stories— City Hall built in the late '20s.

44 top left A native of Italy, Rudolph Valentino epitomized the devastingly handsome, passionate Latin lover. Whether onscreen or off, he caused countless female fans to swoon. If one can believe the tabloids, his leading ladies, too, fell under his spell.

44 center left Another comedian in no need of introduction is Buster Keaton, whose deadpan exterior made his antics all the more hilarious.

44 bottom left Stan Laurel and Oliver Hardy started making movie-goers laugh back in 1927 and their slapstick brand of comedy still proves irresistible today.

44 bottom right Clark Gable, Joan Crawford and Franchot Tone are pictured in a scene from the 1933 musical, Dancing Lady.

44 center Modern Times (1936) is considered one of the greatest films of Charlie Chaplin, who, during his long career, made whole generations laugh and cry.

44 right top Fred Astaire, pictured here in a classic ballroom dance scene with Rita Hayworth. Astaire's technically skilled, lightfooted dance routines were the key ingredient of a series of box-office hits.

44 center right Cary Grant and Ingrid Bergman starred in Alfred Hitchcock's romantic spy thriller, Notorious.

44 bottom right Elizabeth Taylor began her long career at a young age.

45 top left Humphrey Bogart and Lauren Bacall—lovers on screen and married in real life—pictured in a scene from The Big Sleep. *Bogart's death brought their legendary partnership to a sudden tragic end.*

45 center left A young Marlon Brando, as he appeared in The Wild One *(1954). Like Dean, he was considered the archetypal brooding rebel, although he later went on to play a number of famous character roles.*

45 bottom near left Walt Disney.

45 center right James Dean, seen here in Giant *with Liz Taylor. Although Dean made only three films before he was killed in a car crash at age 24, his reputation as a "rebel without a cause" is legendary.*

45 bottom right Marilyn Monroe in the famous publicity shot for Billy Wilder's The Seven Year Itch, *in which she "accidentally" steps over a subway vent, causing her dress to blow up revealingly.*

45 bottom far left and top right John Wayne (left) and Gary Cooper (right): two faces that sum up the world of Westerns. Wayne remained faithful to the stereotype of the fearless cowboy; Cooper instead broadened his range as an actor.

shots, and cross-cutting, i.e. cinema as we know it today. De Mille, on the other hand, was a talented impresario who sensed exactly what the public wanted and made sure they got it. For California, filmmaking was not a pastime but big business. Production companies were funded by Wall Street: behind the scenes big-time financiers made millions while the public ogled at screen stars, from Rudolph Valentino to Theda Bara. By the 20s Hollywood was already an embryonic version of its later self: for moralists, a den of vice; for enthusiastic throngs of cinema-goers, a dream factory; for high-hoping studios, a money-making machine. The advent of sound films, in 1927, was a major turning point, producing a veritable Babel with the invention of the talkies. Values had changed as well: being a star now meant knowing how to speak and perhaps even sing.

The second big crisis for Hollywood and California's filmmaking industry coincided with the arrival in homes of television. Cinemascope, Cinerama, panoramic screens—every possible attempt was made to stem the losses but decline seemed inevitable. Instead California's producers gradually got the message and eventually tied an ever-tighter knot between the two media. Today the film industry receives much of its financing from television. Hollywood has outgrown its hill: the big TV networks have built their studios in the valleys around Los Angeles, and coproductions are more and more frequent. But much of California's and the nation's fascination is still centered—it's true—on Hollywood stars and Oscar night.

Fueled not only by the development of the motion picture, but also by petroleum, manufacturing industries, agriculture, technology, and aerospace, to name a few, California sustained an incredible growth, from 500,000 inhabitants in 1920 to some 31 million today. California's modern-day prospectors now include the venture capitalists who invest in biotechnology, computer technology and real estate developments, among others. Despite its well-publicized troubles of late, the state that spawned the California Dream is still the place where it can come true.

46 left Tom Hanks is one of the new generation of leading men whose role in films has extended beyond acting to active involvement in producing and directing. His performance in Philadelphia *won him the 1995 Oscar award for Best Actor.*

46 right Robert Zemekis (left) and Steven Spielberg teamed up as director and producer to create the box-office smash, Who Framed Roger Rabbit? *They are seen here at the Academy Awards ceremony accepting an Oscar.*

47 bottom right Robert De Niro is seen collecting an Oscar for Best Actor, won for his role as middleweight fighter Jake La Motta in the Martin Scorsese film, Raging Bull.

47 top left Actress Kim Basinger kneeling in front of her newly installed bronze star on Hollywood Boulevard's "Walk of Fame."

47 top right Sharon Stone, seen at a Hollywood affair, became a star overnight thanks to her sizzling role as a seductress in Basic Instinct.

47 bottom left Harrison Ford acquired star status for his role as Indiana Jones, but it was perhaps as the dispirited hunter of androids in the cult film, Blade Runner, *that he gave one of his finest performances.*

48 top right Outlined against the bay in this cityscape is Coit Tower, 210 feet high. The structure was built in 1933 to commemorate the heroism of the city's firefighters.

49 Once home of the local fishing fleet, Fisherman's Wharf is now a favorite tourist haunt. The hub of the area is

Ghirardelli Square, a former chocolate factory where sweet shops still cater to chocoholics.

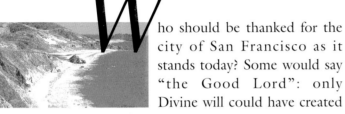

Who should be thanked for the city of San Francisco as it stands today? Some would say "the Good Lord": only Divine will could have created this immense natural harbor, so amazingly well sheltered it escaped the notice of a shrewd explorer like Sir Francis Drake. (He had the misfortune to sail right past it, leaving an indelible blot on his reputation as a navigator.) A business person would say "gold": the Gold Rush of the

mid-1800s led to an influx of immigrants and wealth, heralding future prosperity. A historian would say "the railway": it brought to San Francisco Chinese, Japanese, Scandinavian, Italian, Russian, Greek, Mexican and Filipino immigrants, who have created a vibrant patchwork of ethnic communities that coexist peacefully. The man or woman of letters would say "the museums, theaters, and bookstores": since San Francisco, the West Coast's most European city, vibrates with new ideas, cultural debate and civilized diversions. Artists would say "the Beat generation": however, long before the swinging Sixties, San Franciscans were known to march to the beat of a different drummer. Rudyard Kipling once described the people of San Francisco as delightful and a little bit crazy. At any rate, San Franciscans have a constructive optimism that has turned their city into one of the most livable in the U.S.

48 top left The island of Alcatraz was once a prison for notorious criminals, only two of whom ever attempted escape. The island is now a national monument visited daily by ferry by tourists from all over the world.

48 bottom left The San Francisco Bay is a vital component of the city's landscape.

The Spaniards originally called the place Yerba Buena, after the wild mint that grew in abundance in this compellingly beautiful landscape of rolling hills. In 1776, Father Francisco Palou probably saw the future San Francisco as a promised land, when he founded the Mission Dolores. The mission still stands, on Dolores Street, in sharp contrast to the skyscrapers that crowd the throbbing heart of the city. Some few years ago the high-rise buildings of San Francisco were the subject of a referendum: the populace voted against transforming their corner of paradise into a forest of gleaming spires. They also turned out en masse to oppose "progress" in the form of a highway that would have torn through the urban fabric. In an outburst of civic pride, San Franciscans decided the harbor area, too, was to be protected at all costs.

There was, of course, a price to pay: industry has taken its factories and jobs to more welcoming cities. But the quality of life has benefited incomparably. Today San Francisco is a fairly small city of about 750,000 people (the nearby communities of Oakland, Berkeley, Marin and San Mateo add some 5 million more to the Bay Area). And in the parks, on steep streets meandering up hillsides, in theaters and marketplaces, people seem to live at a less hurried pace than in other large U.S. cities. There's less frenzy and less competition, too. San Francisco is a friendly place where neighbors stop to talk to each other. In this atmosphere of tolerance and

51

52 top left The Golden Gate Bridge was designed by a young American engineer, Joseph B. Strauss. At the time, his project met with both admiration and doubt: it seemed impossible that such a graceful and seemingly delicate structure could withstand the bay's furious currents.

52 center and bottom left Golden Gate Bridge seen from Point Bonita. San Franciscans say that to get the full impact of the bridge's splendor, you must cross it on foot and experience the shaking caused by winds sweeping across the water.

52 right San Franciscans are great sailors, and the winds that come sweeping into the bay, beneath the soaring spans of the Golden Gate Bridge, offer thrills— and occasional spills—for even the most ocean-wise skippers.

53 The bridge that crosses San Francisco Bay where it meets the ocean is crossed daily by some 100,000 vehicles, traveling in six lanes. This feat of engineering can withstand winds blowing at up to 200 miles per hour. Running inside the metre-thick cables are about 75,000 miles of cable: three times the circumference of the equator.

52

cosmopolitan sophistication, San Francisco has also become the home of one of the largest and most integrated gay communities, intensively committed to the fight against AIDS and for civil rights.

Most visitors enter the city by crossing the orange-red Golden Gate Bridge. This highly visible symbol of San Francisco ranked as the world's longest bridge until 1964 (when, with the completion of the Verrazzano Bridge, the Big Apple managed to go one better). The Golden Gate Bridge is undeniably one of the most robust: designed by Joseph B. Strauss and inaugurated in 1937, it has stood up to just about everything in its 60 years. The currents of the Pacific and the 16 rivers flowing into San Francisco Bay have not perturbed it. Nor have the more than 40 million cars and 9 million pedestrians that cross it annually, speeding or strolling from the city to Redwood, and vice versa. Even the bridge's 1000th suicide—a sad record, chalked up in 1995—left California's most famed engineering feat untouched. Two natural elements have, on several occasions, made it tremble. One is the wind. You have only to spend a day in San Francisco to realize that wind here is no gentle breeze. The Golden Gate

Bridge has been closed to traffic three times on account of gale-force blasts. The second natural element is—no surprise here—earthquakes. The violent quake of 1989 put the structure to a severe test, but it came out unscathed—or almost. The strengthening work decreed necessary by the city authorities will in no way change the appearance of the bridge: they know that any alteration would have the people of San Francisco up in arms!

Golden-Gate is also the name of the city's best-loved park, with more than 1,000 acres fronting the ocean. It is the largest city park in the world, with a vast expanse of green lawns, bicycle paths, botanical gardens, sports facilities, and lakes. It also boasts several museums: the California Academy of Sciences, comprising an aquarium and a planetarium; the Asian Art Museum and the M.H. De Young Memorial Museum, with its collections of American art. A short distance from the park is the long shore of Ocean Beach or, in the bay direction, the landmark Fisherman's Wharf. This pier was once the undisputed "territory" of Italian immigrants from Genoa, Sicily, and Naples, who created San Francisco's fishing industry and eventually saw the

54-55 Lincoln Park golf course is just one of the San Francisco's popular public courses. Designed by John McLaren, the park occupies land that was once the site of the Golden Gate Cemetery.

55 top The green meadows of Golden Gate Park were created on land reclaimed from barren sand dunes. Now people come to stroll in the flower gardens, visit museums and enjoy the recreational facilities.

57 top left As the sun drops behind the horizon, Fisherman's Wharf enjoys a moment's calm before the evening influx of tourists and gourmets.

57 top right Times have changed at Fisherman's Wharf: While fishermen of Italian heritage used to sell their catch here, now many Italian-Americans run the area's restaurants, where seafood has pride of place on the menu.

56 Ghirardelli Square, overlooking the bay. A mall, chock-full of stores and restaurants, is now housed in the old chocolate factory, where the machines are kept working to amuse both children and adults alike.

harbor "upgraded" to become one of the city's prime tourist attractions. The aroma of Italy still hangs in the air, in tiny restaurants and trattorias. Nearby shopping malls throng with people at every hour of the day. At the very center of activity is Ghirardelli Square where Italian Domenico Ghirardelli built his dream chocolate factory. A gem of turn-of-the-century taste and technology, the model factory no longer makes chocolate on site but offers other

56-57 Bustling Broadway crosses Pacific Heights, as far as Russian Hill: there it dives into a tunnel and reemerges down by the Embarcadero.

treats to sate your appetite. A nearby area filled with museums testifies to San Francisco's nostalgic tendencies. For anyone who feels the call of the sea, the city's Maritime National Historical Park and Museum abounds with beautifully restored historic vessels, models and related memorabilia. The Cannery, formerly owned by Del Monte, now houses the Museum of the City of San Francisco and provides a venue for visiting performers. Well visible from

the waterfront is Alcatraz Island, named by the Spaniards after its population of pelicans. But the inhabitants eventually changed and its name became synonymous with the high-security federal penitentiary there. Formerly the site of a "presidio" and a military prison, between 1934 and 1963 Alcatraz housed America's most notorious criminals, among them Al Capone, the celebrated "public enemy no. 1." Successful breakouts from Alcatraz were unknown until the stronghold's legendary reputation was challenged by a mysterious escape, subsequently enacted on the screen by Burt Lancaster. And yet a doubt remained, for no trace of the three fugitives was ever found. Who knows . . . maybe the waters of the bay were kind to them, and these one-time inmates of Alcatraz are now enjoying a serene old age.

Not far from the harbor are North Beach, San Francisco's Italian quarter, and nearby Chinatown, the largest Chinese community outside Asia. Early Chinatown had a reputation as a den of vice and opium-smoking. Paradoxically, the 1906 earthquake provided Chinatown with a new lease on life. Razed to the ground, a vibrant new community rose from the ashes, and a tour of its streets today is an exhilarating experience. By the way, it was here, too, that the fortune cookie tradition got started, in 1909. These cookies, which now complement every Chinese meal served in America, are unheard of in China itself.

One of the most characteristic features of San Francisco is its hills (43 in all), judging from the city's sturdy-legged inhabitants and the exhausted expressions of tourists who clamber to the top of Nob Hill or Russian Hill, the steepest mounts in the downtown area. Altitude once served to distinguish between the haves and the have-nots, keeping out those not sufficiently wealthy to have domestic staff (presumably to carry home the shopping) and horses sturdy enough to cope with the inclines. The twisting hairpin turns of Lombard Street—one of the city's most notorious routes to navigate— have made it another San Francisco trademark. Living high on the hill did not remain the prerogative of the wealthy, thanks to an engineer and an earthquake. Andrew Hallidie patented the cog wheel system used by the cable cars that became San Francisco's most characteristic form of transport. Lines still operate today and meet—mere coincidence?—at the top of Nob Hill. Finally more humble folk could, for a few cents, join the aristocrats on the roof of the city. Then the 1906 earthquake destroyed most of the lofty homes of the well-heeled, in one fell swoop—admittedly a traumatic way of restoring topographical democracy.

62 left The Neiman Marcus department store offers a restaurant with a stunning view under an enormous dome of colored glass.

62 right A giant of gleaming glass and steel, the Transamerica Pyramid towers over an old pastel-painted Victorian house on Columbus Avenue.

Unlike sprawling Los Angeles, San Francisco has been kind to its next-door neighbors. Rather than seize and devour, the city has let them rise and shine. Across the stunning Bay Bridge is Oakland, an industrial center. Here San Francisco-born Jack London was raised and began his life of adventure. In the First and Last Chance Saloon, you can still see his favorite table, where he sat writing and, especially, drinking. Also in the East Bay is Berkeley, home of the University of California at Berkeley. A lecture with a cutting-edge thinker or a dance performance is likely to be available. Although life at Berkeley has been

tranquil as of late (except for the occasional Nobel Prize), it was a hotbed of radical dissent against the Vietnam War back in the 1960s. The dean was not surprised that the university was becoming a hotbed of protest: "It's like telling me students like strawberries" was his laconic comment. Today the university campus near the Pacific has about 30,000 students who, on campus and off, enjoy a lively stimulating city with great ethnic restaurants and the best in films, dance, and music concerts that a modern university city could offer.

64 *The towering giants of the Financial District dominate the San Francisco skyline, but at street level, the human scale of the city transpires, and the pace of life has a distinctly European flavor.*

65 top *The opening of the Bay Bridge marked the end of an era; for decades, only ferries had connected the peninsula with Oakland. Traffic crosses the bridge on two levels: the upper for vehicles headed toward San Francisco, the lower for those toward the mainland.*

65 bottom *After dark, the illuminated structure of St. Ignatius is a highly visible landmark. The church of the University of San Francisco, it is still run by the Jesuits who founded it in 1855. This photo was taken from Twin Peaks, hills which dominate the city.*

66-67 and 67 top right Downtown Los Angeles, the city's business district, is a jungle of glass and steel giants built with the latest in anti–seismic technology. During the tremors that all too frequently shake the ground of California, such buildings are designed to sway.

L os Angeles, known as "City of Angels" (from the Spanish), might more properly be called the City of Angles. The downtown has glittering, sharp-edged high rises. Hundreds of miles of boulevards, highways, freeways and expressways intersect each other, criss-crossing what was once barren desert. Angles are even important to the film and fashion industries, where finding just the right angle to frame the shot is a critical skill. So is finding just the right angle to pitch the deal, or sell the concept to the money people. And in L.A., the art of the deal is everything.

Los Angeles has come a long way from September 4, 1781, when a group of 44 settlers of varying ethnic backgrounds (predominantly Spanish) founded it and made it into a small farming village. (They originally named it El Pueblo de la Reina de Los Angeles, which means the town of Our Lady of the Angels.) Today, Greater Los Angeles spreads out over five counties—Los Angeles, Riverside, Ventura, Orange, and San Bernardino covering an area of about 34,000 square kilometres. Its growth has come from many industries, particularly the film, petroleum, citrus, and aerospace industries. And, as it has moved from small village to a thriving megalopolis, its population has become even more ethnically diverse.

Living side-by-side within that five-county sprawl are people from

67 top Chinatown is one of the districts of Los Angeles favored by tourists and residents alike. Bustling and picturesque by day, the atmosphere changes after dark. Then, as its thousands of tiny shops close, countless traditional and modern restaurants, karaoke bars and clubs open their doors, and an upbeat nightlife begins.

66 For stunning views of L.A. and the surrounding areas, the top of City Hall Tower, seat of the local government, is one of the finest vantage points.

67 bottom right Westwood, one of the few neighborhoods in Los Angeles where one might take a leisurely stroll, is the home of the University of California at Los Angeles (or, UCLA).

68 top Even in Los Angeles's financial district, with its forest of futuristic skyscrapers, space has been found for a pedestrian walkway dotted with works of art and shaded by palms.

68 top Even in Los Angeles's financial district, with its forest of futuristic skyscrapers, space has been found for a pedestrian walkway dotted with works of art and shaded by palms.

68-69 Sunlight reflects on the 10,000 glazed panels of Crystal Cathedral in Orange County. The building was designed by architect Philip Johnson, at a cost of $16 million.

every nation on earth. Predominant among them are those of Hispanic, Asian, African and European descent, but there are also Australians and South Americans, as well as Native American descendents of California's original inhabitants. For the most part, Los Angeles' multiethnic residents peaceably share gyms and skateboarding trails, hamburgers and macrobiotic fare. And their different cuisines, cultural celebrations, and traditions give Los Angeles much color, and a worldbeat kind of hipness.

It's also a great stimulant to the arts, which are very much alive in L.A. Within the dance and documentary film communities for instance, are many inspired folks who live to push the envelope a little further. The music scene is just as dynamic, and there are plenty of wanna-be recording artists and comedians who migrate to L.A., hopeful of that big break. Pop culture is also very much at home here (stroll down Melrose Boulevard if you want proof. So are large outdoor murals, which often cover whole walls of large buildings. Most are quite striking.

But nothing has a hold on L.A. quite the way film does. It's probably fair to say that nine out of every ten writers in the region are working on a screenplay, and eighteen out of every 20 waiters, waitresses, and valets could most accurately list "auditioning" as their primary occupation.

As far as large American cities go, Los Angeles is not that easy to navigate. A car is essential, as is a good street map and a basic road map, especially for driving during rush hour. You'll have an easier time getting around if you realize that Los Angeles County is divided into five areas itself: the downtown, the west side, Hollywood, the coast and the valleys.

Downtown, you can walk among tall skyscrapers or old-style adobe neighborhoods, explore a Chinese temple or the hot new art museum. You may even see folks doing their daily t'ai chi exercises on the little grass traffic islands in the heart of the city, especially early in the morning. They may be the only people in L.A. who are not moving at breakneck speed, which is the usual pace here.

If you're curious about the origins of Los Angeles, visit El Pueblo de Los Angeles State Historical Park, on Olvera Street, and stroll on its cobblestone path among 19th-century adobe buildings, soaking up the Mexican flavor. If you'd like to experience Asian culture, wander through Chinatown, as well as Little Tokyo, the cultural, social, and spiritual magnet for Japanese-Americans. Although Californians of Japanese descent were interned as potential spies during World War II, today the influence of Japanese culture is quite pervasive.

Just northwest of the downtown is Hollywood. Movie buffs can stroll along the Walk of Fame on Hollywood Boulevard and gaze at the stars' hand and foot prints at

70 Due to the city's sprawling layout, its said that many Los Angeles residents spend hours each day traveling by car.

70-71 Los Angeles's size alone — 464 square miles — is enough to daunt even the most sophisticated traveler. After dark, it looks like a phantasmagorical tangle of lights, criss-crossed by never-ending ribbons of moving cars, essential possessions in a land where the freeway reigns supreme.

71 top Palm trees contrast with the glistening glass of skyscrapers under a night sky in downtown L.A. Although these tall and majestic trees are part of the L.A. scenery, they were introduced from Florida.

Mann's Chinese Theatre, or venture further west to ogle the fabled mansions of Beverly Hills. (If you want the real low-down on where the celebrities live, consider a bus tour.) Hollywood is so famous worldwide that many people think it *is* Los Angeles, although it is really only one neighborhood among many. And even though most films are now shot elsewhere, Hollywood prevails in the imagination. Spend an afternoon at Universal Studios in Hollywood, and the magic returns. The lights dim, and before you is the somber neo-Gothic house of *Psycho*, the "operating theater" that witnessed the birth of Frankenstein, the daring stuntman dashing into a blazing hotel . . . These stunning special effects catapult you into another reality. Why else would millions of people spend two hours in a darkened room surrounded by strangers, day after day, if not to escape from the real world, even if just for a little while?

If you're hungry, Hollywood has some of the best elegant, upscale restaurants in the city, plus an interesting assortment of inexpensive cafes, burger shops, taco stands, Teriyaki houses, and 50s-style diners. Explore, but be careful, especially at night. Hollywood isn't the safest place.

Wilshire Boulevard, which extends for 18 miles across the city, runs from downtown Los Angeles, through Hollywood, to Westwood, a tony shopping district and home to UCLA, which is clearly the intellectual center of Los Angeles. (UCLA is also famous for its film school; and there are many notable filmmakers who get their start here.) Wilshire Boulevard is one of Los

74 top and 74-75 Santa Monica's sprawling beach — several hundred yards wide — quickly fills with exquisitely tanned bodies, or at least those working toward that goal. Pictured above is the pier. Fishing boats no longer moor here, but crowds of tourists throng its length looking for souvenirs, while gourmets make for the many restaurants. There is even an authentic old carousel, complete with painted wooden horses.

Angeles's main arteries, and the address of several prominent museums, including the La Brea Tar Pits, an intriguing "prehistoric" museum. These pools of water and tar attracted the ancestors of today's largest mammals. Fortunately for us, and unfortunately for them, these mammals sometimes found themselves stuck—forever—to the glue-like pitch beneath the surface. Their fossilized remains, recovered from the pits during systematic excavations started early this century, can now be seen in the museum's showcases.

Also on Wilshire Boulevard is the Los Angeles County Museum of Art. Its outstanding collections, housed in a modular complex, range from Japanese sculpture to Assyrian bas-reliefs, from Titian to Modigliani, from Pre-Columbian jewels to abstract modern art. If you enjoy art or modern architecture, it is definitely worth a visit.

Contributing to Westside's "highbrow" culture are the recently reopened Craft & Folk Art Museum, the Petersen Automotive Museum, the Carole & Barry Kaye Museum of Miniatures and the George C. Page Museum of Discoveries. An even more recent offering is the Museum of Tolerance, at the Simon Wiesenthal Center, which was created to help teach children tolerance and to remind adults to avoid the errors of the past. Its exhibits relate the history of racism and prejudice, and show how they culminated in the horrors of the Holocaust.

In Beverly Hills, Wilshire Boulevard heads due west, parallel to Santa Monica Boulevard, one of dozens of major roads that head straight to the beach. In Los Angeles County, there are more than 60 miles of alluring sands between Malibu and Long Beach, which is a sizable paradise for sun, sea, and sports enthusiasts. But no place along the Los Angeles seaboard can rival the funky town of Venice for sheer color and fun town of Venice is the place to people-watch, and the hangout of rollerbladers, cyclists, jugglers, other street performers, and bodybuilders (who congregate, of course, at Muscle Beach). Street peddlers often have a heyday here, and from their stall-front operations, sell everything imaginable. The cafes that line the boardwalk are very much part of the scene. If you're in Venice, be sure to check out the Rose Cafe, which sells rose-flavored ice cream, and is the watering hole for the local arts community.

Just north of Venice is the quieter, but still upbeat Santa Monica, with its art galleries, antiques stores, trendy cafes, and bookshops. If you're feeling nostalgic for the past, and a little tired of the trendy, find your way to the Santa Monica Pier and explore its delightful turn-of-the-century carousel.

Further north along the coast are wonderful beaches in Topanga and Malibu and lots of trendy shops and cafes. The canyons in Topanga and Malibu, which are inland, are also worth exploring, especially in the spring time when the Santa Monica Mountains are a breathtaking green,

75 California uses its seaboard to full advantage. All year round, aided by the constantly temperate climate, the state's efficiently run marinas and harbors (the one shown in this photo is in Los Angeles) rent out sailing boats, organize ocean fishing trips or provide boats for whale watching trips.

instead of parched brown. Hike if you're feeling adventurous, but at least make the drive. The views are worth it.

South of Venice is Marina del Rey, which is the largest man-made yacht marina in the world. It also houses the picturesque Fisherman's Village, a faithful copy of a New England whaling community.

Inland, large valleys frame the city. They are a world apart from Los Angeles proper, a feeling you'll catch particularly near the top of scenic Mulholland Drive, a curving and fun-to-drive road that cuts through the Santa Monica Mountains and separates the San Fernando Valley from Beverly Hills and points south. Nature predominates along long stretches of Mulholland Drive, which is in sharp contrast to the San Fernando Valley, a sprawling, densely populated conglomeration of smaller suburban cities and towns packed with strip malls, ranch-style homes,

77 top right Sport and fun in Venice with a game of beach volleyball, fiercely fought out on the sands.

76 top and bottom Venice remains one of the most popular beaches in the Los Angeles area. The resort definitely appeals to the biker crowd with their roaring Harley Davidsons, but also swarms with street artists, jugglers, joggers, kids and anyone else who wants to join in the playground atmosphere against a backdrop of trompe-l'oeil decorations and pseudo-Venetian style buildings.

77 top left Although it may not be "politically correct," the bikini contest still flourishes in Hermosa Beach, California.

churches and schools. This is the place that inspired the term "Valley Girls," a slur the women of the area have had to live down ever since.

Burbank, home of the NBC studios (and *The Tonight Show*) is southeast of the San Fernando Valley. Other movie studios are located here as well. Even further east, bordering on the San Gabriel Mountains, is stately Pasadena, famous for its annual Rose Bowl Parade. A bit of the old-time Spanish flavor of Los Angeles lingers in Pasadena still, thanks to the old Hispanic-style architecture of many of the homes.

These are but a few of the highlights of multifaceted, multi-layered L.A., a desert only in the most distant stretches of the imagination. What was once desert now teams with urban life, commerce, art. There's no doubt that L.A. has its share of problems, just like any big city. Cynics say L.A. has four seasons: mudslides, fires, earthquakes and riots. They're right, but so are the dreamers who recognize a different L.A., that mythical, sun-filled Valhalla that promises fulfillment to those who aspire to physical perfection, fadeless youth, fabulous wealth, enduring celebrity, or endless fun.

Where else could you find such a high concentration of beautiful people; their bodies made perfect by long hours at the gym, days of ritual sun-bathing, low-calorie cuisine, and perhaps the crowning touch of a cosmetic surgeon? And where else is conspicuous consumption more brazenly celebrated than on Rodeo Drive?

Clearly, L.A. is a city of contradictions, a place where the J. Paul Getty Museum, a precise reconstruction of the Villa dei Papiri in Herculaneum, can exist almost cheek-by-jowl with dilapidated beach shacks along Pacific Coast Highway. The Getty Museum, the most important privately owned museum in the world, re-creates the atmosphere of ancient Rome at its most sumptuous. The museum's collections include Greek sculpture, and works by Mantegna, Raphael, and Goya. Clearly, the impulse to create beauty permeated Getty's dreams as well, and, multimillionaire

78 top right Sleeping Beauty's Castle in Disneyland, located in Anaheim, is the symbol of a fairy-tale fantasy world.

78-79 Mann's Chinese Theater, with its ornate design, is perhaps the epitome of Hollywood kitsch. Embedded in the sidewalk are long lines of inlaid-bronze stars, inscribed with the names of popular film and TV celebrities. In front of the theater itself are the hand and footprints of such famous stars as Clark Gable and Lana Turner.

79 top No introductions are needed: Minnie and Mickey Mouse offer the same festive welcome for each of the thousands of Disneyland visitors who crowd the world's most celebrated theme park every day.

that he was, he found it easier than most to bring his dreams to fruition.

Eccentrics like Getty have always been welcome in Los Angeles, particularly when they have money to spend, and they raise the bar for others. But, in direct counterpoint to those who were born wealthy or are frenetically driven to accumulate wealth, is a whole subculture of Angelenos who work just hard enough to afford the accoutrements of play. For them, the entire region is one big Disneyland, an "E" ticket ride through the childhood they never want to give up. Fortunately, Los Angeles accommodates them. For those with an hearty appetite for fun, there are more than 60 different amusement parks (each offering countless rides and other pleasures) and 150 resort hotels. Of these, the best known is Disneyland, the large theme park in Orange County. Knotts Berry Farm, the oldest theme park in the United States, is also nearby. While Disney has more action rides, theme lands and the more notable name, the smaller Knotts has a "down-home," authentic ranch-house kind of atmosphere.

For those in the mood for fantasy, the Indiana Jones Adventure or Mickey's Toontown at Disneyland are recent additions to the amusement park scene. In Toontown (inspired by the film *Who Framed Roger Rabbit?*), Donald Duck lives on board a pirate ship. In Goofy's House, absolutely everything is made of rubber and you find yourself bouncing from wall to wall. If that's not enough, try mailing a letter and you'll get a gracious thank-you from the mailbox. And listen for the flowers that sing as you stroll by. You may come away from Toontown weighed down with souvenirs and postcards and sated with junk food, but you'll be convinced you never enjoyed yourself more.

It is offerings such as these that keep most of the folks in the greater Los Angeles area loyal to their region, even when earthquakes shake them up, split their bridges in half, claim lives and make driving to work an arduous marathon. The San Andreas fault that passes right beneath the city is an ever-present reminder that life here is fragile at best, and always unpredictable. So why not pursue fun, or beauty, or wealth? Why not spend long days hiking in the canyons or lolling on the beaches? Or perfecting the Great American screenplay? In Los Angeles, the call to make the most of now, moment-by-moment, is as close as the rumble of nature below.

81 top right A "starlet" poses seductively on an "Angelyne Fan Club" mural. These street decorations are one of many striking features of Los Angeles that catch the eye of tourists.

81 bottom right Another mural on Hollywood Boulevard, this one of two screen stars of totally different fortunes: Bette Davis, whose moviemaking career was long as well as exceptional, and James Dean, an idol whose talents were cut short by a tragic end.

California's oldest city (founded in 1769 by Father Junipero Serra) successfully blends efficiency with Spanish charm, towering skyscrapers with historic Victorian homes. Although its population tops 1.1 million (sixth-largest in the U.S.), San Diego is a vibrant, open city that retains the pleasant, clean, and relatively peaceful feeling of a smaller one. Only a stone's throw from the Mexican border, the desert setting is fringed by the ocean and fanned by sea breezes that temper the heat. The relaxed lifestyle, sunny climate, many attractions, and vestiges of the past make the city a popular destination for visitors year round.

Downtown San Diego marks the place where the city's real growth began and is an ideal place to start a tour of the city. Here, in 1867, businessman Alonzo Horton got things moving after buying a thousand acres of harbor-fronting land overridden with jackrabbits. He had paid only a handful of dollars but the investment was a gamble: initially he had to give land away to get people to build on it. His plucky venture paid off and his name is now emblazoned on Horton Plaza, a grand, upscale consumers' paradise. This multilevel shopping, dining, and entertainment mall was part of a much larger project, designed to upgrade the nearby historic Gaslamp Quarter. The popular area, with its 19th-century landmarks, restaurants and nightlife, has been thoroughly restored (and rescued from its days as the city's red-light district). Not far away is the Embarcadero, a waterfront area that is home to one of the world's most celebrated yacht clubs as well as the Maritime Museum, which has three historic vessels at the heart of its collections. Balboa Park is the centerpiece of San Diego. Its many cultural facilities include the Old Globe Theatre, home of California's oldest professional theater company and the Shakespeare Festival, the Junior Theatre and the famous California Tower, with its resounding chimes. A number of ornate Spanish-Moorish buildings date from an international exposition in 1915. The 1,400-acre park also hosts San Diego's famed zoo, where some 800 species of animals from every corner of the globe roam in exquisitely re-created natural habitats. An aerial tramway crosses above the entire fenced-in area, using hi-tech transport to view the wildlife.

The 2.2-mile San Diego-Coronado Bridge connects mainland San Diego to Coronado Island, with its tony homes, wide beaches, and beautiful vistas. The domes, turrets, towers and carved wood pillars of the elaborate Hotel del Coronado are recognized worldwide, since it was here that Marilyn Monroe, Tony Curtis, and Jack Lemmon lived their hilarious adventures in *Some Like It Hot*. Decorated by the best carpenters of the day (the hotel was inaugurated in 1888), the "Del" is a most unusual beach resort. The very fact that it was built of wood makes it an oddity, since timber was a precious commodity that had to be imported.

The Coronado Bridge offers a great view of the bay. Juan Rodriguez

82 top left The San Diego-Coronado Bay Bridge spans from the mainland to the Coronado peninsula, a garden-city blessed with parks, yacht clubs and the legendary Hotel del Coronado, with its ornate, palatial architecture.

82 top right The ship-like Convention Center (lowest building on the right) overlooks San Diego Bay. The Center's ample facilities incude a huge ballroom, tennis courts, and an amphitheater fronting the sea, plus patios and terraces with wonderful views of the harbor.

82-83 A forest of sail boats, against a backdrop of skyscrapers: San Diego successfully combines the best of business and pleasure, making it one of the most livable cities in the U.S.

84-85 Built near the turn of the century, the swank Hotel del Coronado's circular towers and carved wood pillars make it a favorite San Diego landmark. The hotel's elaborate architecture was seen worldwide in the film Some Like it Hot.

85 top left Founded in 1769 by Father Junipero Serra, Mission San Diego de Alcala was the first Spanish outpost in California. It was moved shortly after in 1774 to distance the church buildings from the military garrisoned at the Presidio.

85 top right The Presidio is located in Mission Valley, where San Diego has its roots. Here, not far from Mission Bay, is the Old Town Historic Park, where authentic old buildings convey vivid impressions of the life of the early settlers.

86-87 San Diego is the sixth-largest city in the U.S. and undeniably one of the most pleasant. Certainly the splendid climate, outdoor lifestyle, and feel-good atmosphere make San Diego a small miracle.

84 top left Balboa Park is a 195-acre area of lush gardens, groves, lakes, and paths. It is also the cultural center of the city, with the Shakespeare Theatre, numerous museums and San Diego's world-famous zoo.

84 bottom left The Casa del Prado, in Balboa Park, was modeled on the chapels of Mexico City Cathedral.

Cabrillo was the first European to sight it, in 1542. He apparently took little notice, surprising since the rocky peninsula of Point Loma forms an magnificent natural harbor. Excavation of the harbor bed has made it possible to accommodate vessels of every shape and size, making San Diego's port a key factor of its thriving economy. Long before the city was built, the shrewd fathers of Mission San Diego already carried on a profitable business with traders from all over the world. Today the piers are crowded with ferries and tourists' yachts, fishing boats, and naval vessels. But you need go no further than the southern tip of Point Loma to rediscover the impressive view first encountered by Cabrillo. Presiding over the ocean is the old lighthouse, a prime spot from which to watch the annual migration of the whales on their way south from Alaska to Baja California.

If San Diego is considered the birthplace of California, then the birthplace of the city is Mission San Diego de Alcala, the first mission to be built in this part of the continent. In the 18th century the missions also put up travelers, and the tradition lives on in Mission Valley, which has the highest concentration of hotels in the city. The Old Town is here, too, with authentic adobe buildings as a visible record of San Diego's history. This historic area is a living museum, with carefully preserved examples of old buildings juxtaposed with "Early California" restaurants and souvenir shops. Oddly enough, the buildings happily coexist. San Diego (like its namesake) has worked a miracle, which is repeated in nearby Victorian-style Heritage Park, where inns still provide wayfarers with food and lodging. North of downtown is Mission Bay, a former swamp that was reclaimed to create the land and huge lagoon that became the core of Mission Bay Park, a mecca for visitors of all ages. Its biggest attraction is Sea World, the marine park famous for its otters, beavers, walruses, penguins, and, especially, the shows where Shamu, the killer whale, and dolphins perform in gigantic pools.

Within the city confines is the stunning coastline and upper-crust community of La Jolla, "the jewel," which certainly offers sights worth seeing. Perhaps most precious of all is the Scripps Institute of Oceanography. Its aquarium museum, plus the San Diego-La Jolla Underwater Park, are prestigious institutions for oceanographic research and places where younger generations learn respect for the marine environment and its creatures. Also important are the Mingei International Museum of World Folk Art, promoting awareness of the world's varied cultures, and the San Diego Museum of Contemporary Art. Another face of La Jolla is seen at the Golden Triangle: not only a shopper's paradise, it is one of the best points from which to admire legendary sunsets over the Pacific.

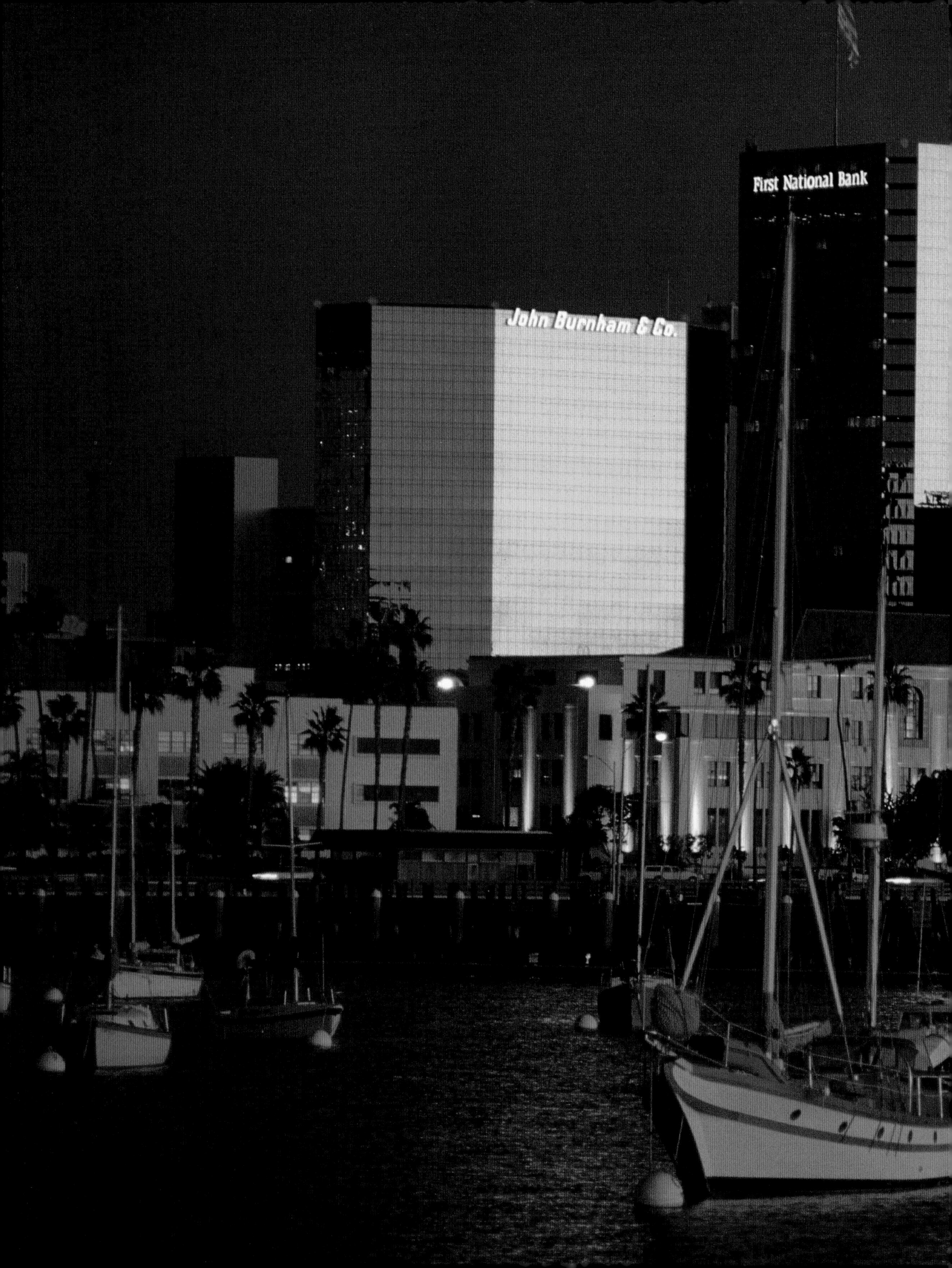
First National Bank
John Burnham & Co.

NATURE

88 top Like other natural treasures, Nevada Falls in Yosemite Park owes much to the determined battles fought by naturalist John Muir. Thanks to Muir, perhaps the first environmentalist, the extraordinary beauty and power of these waterfalls have been preserved intact.

88 center Deer live peacefully in Yosemite Park, in the mountains of the Sierra Nevada range. The park's name apparently derives from the word used by Miwok Indians for the large grizzly bear.

When it comes to natural beauty, California is well endowed. Who could forget the ride along the northerly stretches of Pacific Coast Highway, green cliffs reaching toward the clouds, cows grazing in tranquil pastures? Or Malibu Canyon after the first spring rain? Or the wildflowers that blanket the Northern California countryside soon after the thaw?

As lush as these are, California has landscapes that are just as stark—Death Valley and the Mojave Desert for instance, or the endless flat and featureless stretches in the Central Valley. Few states can boast such variety. But California, quite generously, lays it all out for you with snow-capped mountains and sunny beaches, canyons tufted with tall grasses, dark woods dense with lichen and ferns.

Like the landscape, the climate also tends toward extremes. Up north in the Sierras are mountains that are always snow-covered, and the towns surrounding them seem to suffer from a permanent chill. In the redwood forests of northern California, the weather is often rainy and damp. But the desert air in the southern California is dry and the heat can be intense. And in the Central Valley, the climate is more moderate, making conditions are just right for growing fruits and vegetables.

One of the reasons you find such variety here is that California is quite large. If you were to drive south, from the California-Oregon border, to Mexico, you'd cover roughly the same distance between New York and Indiana. The other factor responsible for the varied topography is this: geologically speaking, California is in its adolescence. And like an adolescent, it is coping with the trauma of physical development and waiting for its permanent adult shape to emerge. Earthquakes and volcanic eruptions continue to influence its topography.

Why are earthquakes so prevalent in California? The culprit is the San Andreas Fault, and the real trouble lies near Big Sur, just north of Monterey. Here, deep below the surface, two huge blocks of the earth's crust face one another. On one side is the tectonic plate that carries the Pacific Ocean and much of coastal California. It's edging northwards at the rate of about 2 inches a year, seemingly ready to play bumper cars with the other block, the North American continent.

The San Andreas fault extends 9 miles into the earth and varies in width, from a few yards to about one mile. It also spawns scores of smaller faults that cause the thousands of quakes recorded in California each year. Every now and again a major earthquake brings tragedy. In 1906, an earthquake brought almost complete destruction to San Francisco, which was hit once again in 1989. The 1994 earthquake that originated in Northridge in Southern California was so severe it was felt

88 bottom Californians who dare to brave the thrills of white-water rafting find the ultimate setting in Sierra Nevada. This photo shows a descent from Clavey Falls, on the Tuolumne River.

88-89 The largest mountain lake in North America, Lake Tahoe holds so much sparkling, clear water that every American could drink 20 gallons of it a day for five years before it would run dry.

89 top The basin of the Merced river, one of the main rivers flowing down from the Sierra Nevada, was carved by a glacier. The valley, formed by the process of erosion, is over 1,000 yards deep.

90 California's
deserts are many
and varied. Since
ancient times, man
has found ways of
surviving amid
these seemingly

boundless rocky
wasteland, while
archaeological finds
confirm that the
first "settlers"
arrived here some
20,000 years ago.

91-92-93-94 Wind
and sand combine to
form the surreal dunes
and undulations in
Death Valley
National Park. Not
all the park is sandy

desert, however: its
region includes both
high (over 9,000 feet)
and low desert areas,
and therefore a great
variety of plant and
animal life.

95 Another view of
Death Valley, showing
just how dry its
terrain can be.
Thousands of years
ago, however, lakes
covered much of this
desert. When they
dried up, native
settlers moved higher
up toward the
mountains, but the
desert was never
completely abandoned.

98-99 Death Valley's geological history has made its stark terrain a unique spot on earth. Here the temperature can soar to 130° F., rain — on the rare occasions when it falls — evaporates immediately, and there is no evident sign of vegetation. Nevertheless, this eerie setting is host to numerous forms of plant and animal life which have managed to adapt well to the extreme conditions of the valley.

99

wines include Chardonnay, Riesling, Pinot Noir, Cabernet Sauvignon, Merlot, and Sauvignon Blanc.

The history of Californian wine goes back a long way, to the days of the Franciscan friars who founded the missions along the Camino Real. In theory, they planted only enough vines to produce the wine needed for their sacraments but—as everyone knows—anything worth its salt will soon find a market, and when fine-quality grape-stock started to arrive from Europe, the Californian wine-growing industry really took off.

Prohibition struck a crippling blow for wine producers in the '20s, and recovery took a long time. In the period immediately following World War II, however, production reached a commendable level: 4 million hectolitres. The Napa Valley is especially fruitful, and its output is cause for concern among European wine growers, who have seen their market share erode.

And the quality is no longer in question. Wine connoisseurs acknowledge that California wine has come of age. The ultimate accolade came in 1985 at a White House dinner held in honor of the Prince and Princess of Wales. The wine served was an '81 California Chardonnay.

California's wine country is particularly picturesque, and the wineries themselves can take some of the credit, although not all. Most are situated in restored old buildings, with tasting rooms that could be mistaken for the salons of French

100 left top and bottom The Joshua tree, actually a tree-like plant, was named by early settlers. The sight of its branches stretched heavenward made them think of the biblical hero, his arms upraised in prayer. The desert area where these plants grow, the Joshua Tree National Monument, is now designated a nature preserve.

100 top right, 100-101, and 101 top Palm Springs offers remarkable evidence of how man can transform a desert into a lush green oasis. This popular vacation spot is a mere two-hour drive from Los Angeles. It owes its existence to the discovery of hot springs and the diversion of the Colorado River, allowing the creation of gardens, parks, and golf courses.

chateaus. And special legislation bans the construction of tacky-looking, fiberglass-reinforced concrete buildings, a concession, perhaps, to the tourism industry that thrives here. That's fortunate, because the wine country does have a romantic look that's worth preserving.

One excellent way to take it all in is to board the Napa Valley Wine Train, which tours the whole region. You'll see many of the hundreds of wineries located in Napa alone, as well as charming Victorian and California-style bungalow homes.

The town of Sonoma, which is further east, has its own charm. Every fall, there's a large wine and arts festival in the town square, fronted by an old Spanish mission and adobe homes. General Vallejo's home is preserved here, too. Glen Ellen, which is just north of Sonoma, houses the lovely Jack London State Park, as well as the remains of his dream home. Sonoma is sometimes called Valley of the Moon, after the title of one of London's books.

102 left There are over 150 vineyards in the Napa Valley and the wines grown here include Cabernet Sauvignon, Chardonnay, Riesling, and Bordeaux. The valley's climate — dry heat during the day, ample moisture at night — is ideal for growing grapes.

102-103 The vineyards of the Napa and Sonoma valleys are relatively new additions to the American landscape. Initially regarded as a curiosity, California's wines are now considered some of the finest in the world.

Besides wine, the North Bay is noted for its redwood preserves, including those in Redwood National and State Park. Redwood National Park is classified by UNESCO as part of mankind's natural heritage. It contains three of the world's tallest redwoods and harbors much wildlife, including black bears, mountain lions, lynx, raccoons and 300 species of birds.

For anyone not familiar with these impressive trees, a few words should be said about the coastal redwood (sequoia sempervirens) and the closely related Sierra redwood (also called big tree or giant sequoia). Although coastal redwoods can tower to heights of over 300 feet (with trunks over 12 feet in diameter), they have shallow root systems and draw moisture from the air through their leaves. The coastal redwoods of the Redwood National Park thrive on the area's winter rains and year-round cooling fog. The giant sequoia flourishes inland, however, in scattered groves on the western slopes of the Sierra Nevada. Native Americans used to revere the trees as dwelling-places of spirits.

Controversies still rage about the harvesting of majestic redwoods and old-growth forests, but the environmental awareness that developed in the late 60s has paid off handsomely here, putting the park at the forefront in the conservation of California's natural assets. Visiting its stands of tall trees can be an almost mystical experience.

Nature also expresses itself gloriously in the Sierra Nevada, the snow-covered mountain range which forms a high ridge extending down the eastern side of California. Here you'll find attractions such as Mount Shasta, Lake Tahoe, and Lassen Volcanic National Park.

On the slopes of the Sierra—and here alone—grow giant sequoias, towering to heights of 300 feet with 30-foot-thick trunks, the largest of all trees in bulk. Visitors come here in search of fresh air and rejuvenation. Mark Twain particularly praised the relaxing and renewing effects of these environs, saying that three months spent on Lake Tahoe could resuscitate even an Egyptian mummy.

Lake Tahoe sits astride the California-Nevada border and may be what remains of an immense Ice Age crater. Another theory about its origins is that lava blocked the water, forming a basin. It's a very deep basin for sure, with a depth of almost 2,000 feet. Someone calculated that, if all the water were drained and

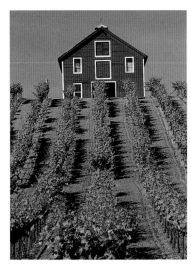

103 top left Three highly rated wine-growing areas— the Alexander, Dry Creek, and Russian River valleys — converge at Healdsburg, attracting wine connoisseurs from all over the world.

103 top right In autumn, the leaves of the trembling poplar turn gold and red. This photo was taken at Lake Sabrina in the Sierra Nevada.

104 top left When the water level of Mono Lake drops, its surface becomes a surreal landscape populated by strange stalactite-like formations. These cylindrical deposits form when calcium-rich-fresh water springs gush into the lake and mix with its alkaline salt water.

104 bottom left The trunk of a giant sequoia, a large evergreen tree, can be as large as 30 feet in diameter and, in exceptional cases, can become even larger. General Sherman Tree, for example, in Giant Forest, has a 35-foot diameter and measures 175 feet around its base.

104 right In 1914, Lassen Peak —now Lassen Volcanic National Park — began to erupt and lava continued to flow from its craters until 1921, destroying huge areas of forest. Mt. Lassen is one of the few active volcanos in the country.

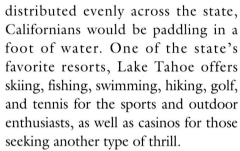

distributed evenly across the state, Californians would be paddling in a foot of water. One of the state's favorite resorts, Lake Tahoe offers skiing, fishing, swimming, hiking, golf, and tennis for the sports and outdoor enthusiasts, as well as casinos for those seeking another type of thrill.

In Yosemite National Park, nature reveals natural splendors that attract some 2.5 million visitors a year. Yosemite Falls is one of the world's highest and most awe-inspiring waterfalls: Upper Yosemite Fall drops 1,430 feet (nine times the height of Niagara), the Lower, 320 feet. Including the cascades in between, the total drop is 2,425 feet: a truly spectacular sight. Here, too, towering El Capitan forms the world's largest block of granite. The passing seasons reveal other sides of the park's infinitely changing face, when winter turns the landscape into a huge cathedral of ice or when spring thaw brings new life to vegetation and awakens animals from hibernation. Alas, Yosemite has become so popular it is in danger of being "loved to death," which may lead the Park Service to introduce measures to reduce the number of cars and visitors.

Sequoia National Park is host to grand old men of American politics and the military: General Sherman, General Lee, Abraham Lincoln, to mention but a few. These are in fact the names of giant sequoias: ancient, colossal trees impervious to parasites or disease, towering skyward like go-betweens of earth and heaven. The park is a paradise for hikers, with trails winding for over 40 miles around groves of giant trees, including some of the loveliest and most majestic in North America. Scottish naturalist John Muir was the "father" of this park, and in the late 1800s he fought hard to preserve the big trees from the lumber companies. Sequoia National Park, together with other areas he saved from destruction, is the finest monument to the strength and courage of a single man.

In the northern part of the state between Sacramento and the Oregon border, the Sierra Nevada Mountains gradually meld into the Cascade Range. Here a totally different scenario awaits you in the Lassen Volcanic National Park, which is not unlike Yellowstone Park with its countless geysers, pools of bubbling

104-105 The groves of trees in Redwood National Park resemble immense natural cathedrals. Their trunks soar like Gothic pillars to heights of over 100 feet before branching out to form a vault of foliage often too thick to be penetrated by the sun.

105 top The peak of Mount Whitney can be seen towering over the hundreds of lakes and rivers that cross Inyo National Forest. Palisade Glacier, on the boundary with Kings Canyon National Park, is the southernmost glacier in the U.S.

mud, fumaroles, and sulfurous springs. Mount Lassen last erupted in 1914, in spectacular style, with ashes spewing as far as Nevada. In 1916, the area was made a national park, one of the smallest and most unusual in the state of California. Trails lead all the way to the Cinder Cone crater. Encompassed by a sea of lava, it's a stirring testimony to the fickle nature of the earth's crust. Looming over all at the top of the state is the mystical Mt. Shasta, which one writer described as "lonely as God and white as a winter moon." The Native Americans revered the mountain for its spiritual force, and modern New Age types consider it a "power point" on the earth's surface.

California's desert regions are centered in Death Valley and span the Mojave and Sonoran deserts from the borders of Nevada and Arizona, extending toward the cities of Los Angeles and San Diego. Vast desert areas feature dissimilar climates and landscapes: in some rain is an exceptional event, others even experience snowfalls. This variety supports numerous species of animal and plant life, all of which have developed sophisticated ways of ensuring their survival. Jackrabbits use their ears as cooling systems; small rodents derive water from seeds they eat; perennial plants have long roots to reach groundwater deep in the subsoil; cacti have leaves with a waxy coating to prevent moisture evaporating. This fascinating world is best observed unhurriedly and with the aid of an

107 bottom The sun rises on the sheer granite walls and canyons of Kings Canyon National Park, one of the most spectacular wilderness sites in the state.

108-109 Bristlecone pines, the longest-living conifer known, still grow in the White Mountains region. These gnarled trees, unaffected by extreme weather conditions, are thought to be about 4,500 years old, making them the oldest trees on earth.

experienced guide, for deserts can also play unkind tricks, with effects as disorienting as cactus wine.

Death Valley is the hottest, driest place in California. Early immigrants heading for gold country paid dearly for taking a shortcut here: in the lowest point in the valley, 280 feet below sea level, it is not unusual for the temperature to climb above 125°F. Yet California's highest peak—Mount Whitney, 14,000-feet high—is only some 40 or so miles away. The valley owes its arid climate to the Sierra Nevadas, which shield it from rain. The burning sun and barren terrain create lunar landscapes and variegated colors—ochre, gray, white, yellow—that enhance the spectacle. Having learned a lesson from the gold seekers, summertime visitors rarely stir from their air-conditioned vehicles and carry sufficient fuel and water to get them as far as Furnace Creek, a village-cum-oasis. Here are the only pools to be seen in these parts, containing water as hot as a thermal spring.

In spite of its climate, severe environmental conditions and an overwhelming sense of emptiness, Death Valley sustains 600 species of plant life, many different mammals, birds, and even fish. Humans have even succeeded in exploiting its resources, mining borax, the desert's "white gold," instead of the far more precious yellow gold that a few obstinate individuals persist in searching for.

The desert also needs protecting: as we have seen, it is not solely an austere wasteland of sand and rock, to be exploited for mineral deposits or used as sets for movies. California's desert is—among other things—a unique source of archeological finds, all the more precious in a region where every fragment of history is of vital importance. Rock paintings and artifacts dating as far back as 20,000 years could tell a lot about the Native Americans who lived here long before the arrival of the Spanish conquistadors. Sad to say, attempts to make the deserts protected areas have met with little success. Meanwhile sprawling cities continue to grow, endangering a fragile and delicately balanced ecosystem, placed in jeopardy by the very slightest interference.

Californians enjoy a stupendous outdoor playground, which they take full advantage of: whether walking in the desert at night, peering at the bright bowl of stars, camping at a remote mountain lake, listening to the cry of birds; hiking past colorful flowers in high alpine meadows, or observing a bald eagle or a peregrin falcon maneuver in the sky. Enjoying the outdoors is also as accessible as rollerblading in a scenic spot, playing volleyball on the beach, basking in the sun in a small private beach cove.

112 top left Windsurfing is a favorite sport of native Californians, geared to sun, sea, fitness, and fun.

112 top right La Jolla, is one of the chicest and most beautiful residential areas outside San Diego. Its attractions include Scripps Institute of Oceanography, one of the world's leading science institutions in this field, and San Diego-La Jolla Underwater Park.

112-113 One of the countless California surfers braving the Pacific waves.

113 Sea World, at Mission Bay in San Diego, is a 24-acre marine amusement park, the largest structure of its kind in the world. Millions of visitors show up each year to catch a glimpse of such marine mammals as penguins, dolphins, seals, sea lions, and whales.

One of the most celebrated features of the Golden State is its 840 miles of glorious shoreline, kissed by the sun, lapped by gentle waves or pounded by frothing surf. A walk, jog or drive along the coast offers startlingly beautiful scenery: natural harbors and cliffs soaring high above the sea, stunning nature reserves, trees twisted by the wind, playful dolphins. A meeting place of land and sea—as Robert Louis Stevenson described it—against a backdrop of rocky headlands . Depending how the mood takes you, your journey can be geared to fitness, culture, or simple contemplation—or a combination of all three. Our coastal itinerary travels from south to north, starting in sunny San Diego at Point Loma, the peninsula that protects the city's harbor from Pacific waves and tides. At this southwesternmost tip of continental America, you can pay tribute to the discoverer of the West Coast at the Cabrillo National Monument or take in stunning views of the rugged cliffs and harbor from a 144-acre park. But the most popular activity around these parts, from December to mid-March, is whale-watching: pods of gray whales—as many as 12,000—pass this way each year when migrating to Baja California. Just a 15-minute drive north of San Diego is another convenient place for whale-watching, Whale Point in La Jolla, a place where the shoreline can resemble an unspoiled stretch of the Cote d'Azur.

Much more about the life and habitat of these marine mammals can be learned at the city's Oceanographic Institute, a top place for children, who can experience close encounters with these friendly sea creatures.

The California surfing obsession is very much in evidence around these parts. Oceanside, north of San Diego, is celebrated for the surf championships held here annually. Once a propitiatory rite of Polynesian kings, surfing was introduced into California at the beginning of the century. The Pacific coast offers an ideal place for this sport, and for surfing fanatics there is even a phone number to call for up-to-the-minute information on sea conditions, height and "quality" of the waves.

Even in Los Angeles, mind and body can be equally well restored on the long white beaches of Santa

114-115 Heading south from Big Sur towards Los Angeles, the wild, rugged coast gives way to stretches of shoreline interspersed with long, pleasant beaches — ideal for barefoot strolling — in bays protected from the mightier Pacific waves.

116-117 A sea lion basks in the sun on San Miguel, one of five islands off the coast of Santa Barbara that form the Channel Islands National Park. San Miguel is the only island in the world where the presence of six different species of pinniped, a type of aquatic mammal, has been recorded.

116 top A view of the magnificent Anacapa Islands, a chain of three small islands close to the coast popular with vacationers.

117 top Santa Cruz, the largest of the Channel Islands: access to this island, too, is regulated by the park's administrating authority. Long ago, the archipelago was a single, large island: the level of the sea has risen 300 feet since then.

117 center and bottom The shores of the Channel Islands are the natural habitat of thousands of marine mammals. Sea lions and seals (including the huge elephant seal) are often spotted here.

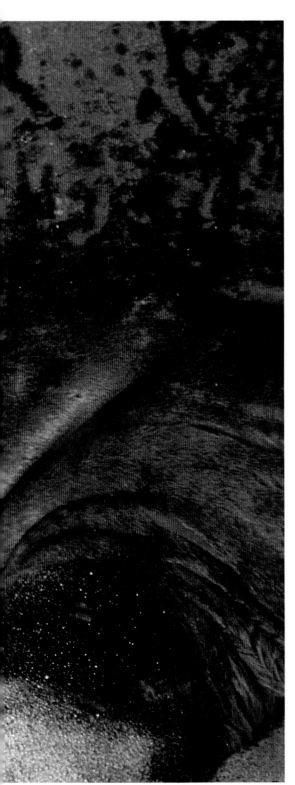

Monica and its bay, immortalized in millions of postcards. For Angelenos and tourists in search of paradise, this is Eden. Santa Monica State Beach is considered one of the finest in the Los Angeles area. It starts here and winds along 20 miles of coastline past Malibu. The latter, of course, is California's legendary celebrity colony, where the scene includes inaccessible villas, ultra-luxury hotels and gleaming Harley Davidsons. The Pacific Coast Highway (Route 1) runs

118-119 *An incomparably beautiful stretch of coastline not far from Monterey Bay, Big Sur fired the imagination of writers like Robert Louis Stevenson and John Steinbeck. Its scenic cliffs and coves are favorite haunts of California's nature-lovers.*

parallel to the ocean, past beaches and missions. Sometimes the seaboard towns have famous names, and sometimes the highway thrusts inland, revealing a still unspoiled corner of America.

When in the Los Angeles area, break away from the coast to take in attractions of a totally different kind in Palm Springs, less than 100 miles away. Famed as the super-resort of the American desert, it is a magnetic draw for vacationers. Visitors throng here from as far away as Europe to savor the ambience created by the rich and famous who have built sumptuous homes here. And if the 50,000 palm trees planted to enhance the desert scenery and the many pools do not relieve the torrid heat of summer (up to 100°F), try a visit to Mount San Jacinto or explore the Joshua Tree National Monument. This vast desert preserve was named after the famous Joshua trees, which are giant yuccas. In the desert oasis of Palm Springs more than 1 million gallons of water a day are used to keep the city's golf courses green (there are over 70). Golf is, after all, just part of the daily routine for residents of this Shangri-La.

Ventura, halfway between L.A. and Santa Barbara, is a good place to embark on a trip to the Channel

119 Malibu, north of Santa Monica, is famous for both its magnificent beaches and extravagant mansions. It is also host to the world-renowned J. Paul Getty Museum, a re-creation of the Villa of Scrolls in Herculaneum, which is endowed with one of the richest art collections in the entire world.

Islands, an archipelago of seven volcanic islands. Extraordinarily rich in fauna, the islands have been called the American Galapagos. Ventura's sights include the San Buenaventura Mission, high on the hills; wooden homes in pastel colors and the Historical Museum, where visitors are reminded that Native Americans lived here long before the missions were built.

The city surely blessed by every known deity is Santa Barbara. A thoroughly Spanish charm pervades its streets, with Moorish-style buildings and fragrant gardens surrounding homes owned by Michael Douglas, Michael Jackson, Ronald Reagan, and the like in the exclusive Montacito district. Every minor detail of the street furnishings —down to trash bins and mailboxes encased in Spanish tile—points to obsessive concern with preserving architectural homogeneity.

The hundreds of joggers and rollerbladers thronging the Cabrillo Bikeway, 20 miles of palms and green lawns, exude a certain Californian love of life and a self-confident fitness. Essential sites for tourists on the trail of local history are Santa Barbara's old Spanish buildings. The most noteworthy are Mission Santa Barbara, founded in 1786 and considered California's finest, and the County Courthouse, a castle in Moorish style decorated with murals, ceramics and intarsia work, built after the 1929 earthquake.

The appeal of the Central Coast —the 250 miles of shoreline between

Santa Barbara and Carmel—lies in its spectacular and varied landscapes, from the unashamed opulence of Santa Barbara to the mystical tranquillity of Big Sur. An unusual Pacific experience can be had at Pismo, where Californians race their motorbikes across 21 miles of golden sand dunes, under the watchful eye of rangers. If one detours to venture inland, mirage-like Solvang is a corner of Scandinavia transported to California, with Danish-style buildings, windmills, and street names, put here by settlers who founded the village in the early 1900s.

The route to San Luis Obispo passes through meadows and hillsides dotted with vineyards. Mission San Luis Obispo de Tolosa, the fifth to be built in California, points to the city's

122 top left A front view of Casa Grande, the main house at Hearst Castle at San Simeon, which was modeled after Seville Cathedral. Newspaper magnate William Randolph Hearst began work on this enormous estate in the 1920's; it was still unfinished when he died some 30 years later.

colonial past. However, the main attraction in the area is a farm tour: here they produce and sell everything under the sun, from almonds and zucchini to cheese. Returning to the crashing waves and surf of the Pacific, one finds Morro Bay, one of the foremost wildlife sanctuaries in California. Here birdwatchers can watch peregrine falcons circling high above Morro Rock. A now-endangered species, the bird nests on this volcanic cliff towering 600 feet above the bay.

The volcanic rock beach of Cayucos has few diversions to offer, unless you are following the legendary trail of James Dean, who perished in his metallic Porsche just 25 miles from Paso Robles, now known mainly for its almond orchards. On the other hand, Hearst Castle, built by tycoon William Randolph Hearst at San Simeon, is an over-the-top monument to opulence: collections of artworks from every corner of the globe are displayed beneath splendid intaglio ceilings, imported from monasteries all over Europe.

Millionaires' extravaganzas and amusements parks are in short supply after heading north from San Simeon (though you may chance to hear some picturesque tales about an old village's former whaling days). Yet thousands of people are lured to drive along this road, climbing up to Big Sur and beyond, to reach Monterey Bay. The twists and turns follow the jagged shoreline, across scenery that holds all the fascination of nature in the raw. Big Sur is rugged countryside which—as Californian poet Robinson Jeffers put it—only a fallen meteorite could plow. But for Henry Miller this is the face of the earth as the Creator intended. It is in any case a not-to-be-missed experience for intellectuals, artists, and anyone

hoping to commune with the Creative Spirit in canyons replete with redwoods and along semideserted bays. The scattered residents (hardly more numerous than in the early 1900s) keep a jealous watch over their territory, much of which is private — California urbanization gets short shrift here.

In Carmel, at the southern base of the Monterey peninsula, one finds a bohemian atmosphere in an upscale setting. Local ordinances forbid high-rise buildings, neon signs, normal-sized street signs, and even mailboxes (mail has to be collected from the central office). The locals in their attractive cottage homes are proud of their village, since the late 1800s a favorite haunt of artists and intellectuals. Carmel's detractors claim the city's soul has been sold to the devil of tourist speculation, but Carmel stoically withstands all attacks.

Along the Seventeen-Mile Drive, the scenic route that winds around the Monterey Peninsula, crossing Del Monte Forest, one can spy mansions built here in the 1920s. Today, anyone not in a position to tee off on one of the countless golf courses of exclusive Pebble Beach can make the most of a public beach near Pacific Grove. If you are lucky, you will witness one of nature's most spectacular sights: thousands of monarch butterflies, their wings outspread in the sun, wintering among the eucalyptus trees. It's a surrealistic picture affording a foretaste of the charm of Monterey

126 top Mission San Carlos Borromeo del Rio Carmelo was founded in Monterey in 1770 and relocated to Carmel four years later. The stone church is surrounded by carefully tended gardens containing a fountain.

126-127 The
Monterey peninsula is
a realm of wildlife
sanctuaries and
dazzlingly white
sands, with the added
appeal of Spanish
traditions and
exclusive beach resorts.
Golf is popular here,
especially when played
on one of the
numerous courses in
and around Pebble
Beach.

126 top and bottom
The thick vegetation
of Pebble Beach,
north of Carmel,
conceals luxury
mansions and
famous golf courses.
Pictured in the photo
below is the Lone
Cypress, scanning the
ocean from its clifftop
site.

and its bay, which was discovered in 1542 by the Portuguese navigator Juan Rodriguez Cabrillo. Especially in spring and summer coastal fog envelops these nearly 60 miles of shoreline but does not discourage tourists in search of peace and quiet.

The bay's most amazing sights are underwater. Canyons deeper than Arizona's lie beneath the waves, alive with seals, sea otters, sea lions, and thousands of microscopic forms of plant life. The huge marine valley here discovered by George Davidson in 1890 is considered by marine biologists one of the richest places in the world. This undersea environment can also be explored on dry land in the Monterey Bay Aquarium, one of the largest in the U.S. The aquarium resides on Cannery Row, the street immortalized by John Steinbeck in his book of the same name. The smell of sardines has long gone, together with the packing plants, replaced by the tourists who now throng Fisherman's Wharf. With its picturesque restaurants and noisy fish-markets, it is the only crowd-pulling historic site with a claim to authenticity.

Situated on the northern lip of Monterey Bay is the city of Santa Cruz, whose tranquil spirit and tourist orientation were severely

128 top *Some 30 miles north of San Francisco, Point Reyes National Seashore is a coastal park covering an area of 26,000 acres: hundreds of miles of trails wind up and down its craggy headlands and windswept beaches.*

128-129 *The beach at Pescadero, south of San Francisco, a haven for many species of birds. The name apparently refers to the fish with which the waters of the bay once teemed, and is now a paradise for bird watchers.*

129 top An aerial view of Drake Bay and its nearby estuary.

129 center Memorial Church is one of the architectural features of Stanford University campus in Palo Alto, not far from San Francisco. The university was founded by Leland Stanford, a railroad tycoon.

129 bottom Silicon Valley is named after one of the most-used materials in the manufacture of electronic components. Home to an enormous number of high-tech companies, it is spread throughout the southern end of the San Francisco Bay.

130-131 An impressive panoramic view of the Californian coastline, highlighting the extremes of its landscapes: verdant hills offer a startling contrast to desolate cliffs and canyons— magnficent scenery that has fired the imagination of artists and writers.

shaken but not destroyed by the 1989 earthquake. The hills around are populated by the whiz kids of electronics, the young turks of Silicon Valley. The name, by the way, describes a phenomenon, not a place: the concentration of the world's most highly advanced technology in the county of Santa Clara, south of San Francisco Bay. In Silicon Valley some of the most brilliant alumni of Stanford and Berkeley universities have turned the American dream into reality, conquering professional and financial success in one of the 3,000 high-tech electronics businesses that have sprung up since the late 1970s. The fruit once grown here in huge quantities has been replaced by office buildings, microprocessors, pocket calculators, cordless phones and lasers. In contrast to state-of-the-art lifestyles and relentless "progress," public opinion here has begun to challenge ever-rising growth rates in an area now at the saturation point. Take the case of record breaking San José, the fastest-growing city in the world. It is a city without a soul—some say, competing against itself in the race to equip its airport by the end of the century with facilities to handle 12 million passengers.

North of San Francisco, beyond the upscale town of Sausalito, the urban landscape recedes and nature takes over again. The air becomes moist with the rain and fog that help eucalyptus trees to thrive here, and the wind-swept coast gets wilder.

Mendocino is almost an apparition, with its Victorian architecture and the huge Headlands State Park overlooking the ocean. Loved by artists and bohemians, surrounded by fields where California poppies burst into color in spring, it is the elegant gateway to the Avenue of Giants.

The mammoths in question are redwoods, for decades the key to the prosperity of Northern California, although today lumbering the redwoods is subject to environmental restrictions. On the far side of Eureka—more timber-built houses, Queen Anne style mansions, sawmills—the coastal strip is covered with towering trees as far as the Oregon boundary. The journey which started with the whales of San Diego ends in the silence of Trinidad Bay, protected by redwoods, the gentle giants.

INDEX

MUSEUM AND ART COLLECTIONS

London—National Portrait Gallery: page 24 bottom right.

Rotterdam—Marine Museum: page 24 bottom, left.

Vincennes—Marine History Department: pages 22-23, 23 top, 26-27.

ILLUSTRATION CREDITS